ADIRONDACK
GHOSTS
III

ADIRONDACK GHOSTS III

Historic Haunts in
New York State's North Country

LYNDA LEE MACKEN

ADIRONDACK GHOSTS III
Historic Haunts in New York State's North Country

Published by
Black Cat Press
P. O. Box 1218
Forked River, NJ 08731
www.lyndaleemacken.com

ISBN 978-0-9755244-9-7

Book & Cover Design by Deb Tremper, Six Penny Graphics.
www.sixpennygraphics.com

Printed in the United States of America by Sheridan Books, Inc.
www.sheridanbooks.com

Dedication

To Mary and George Baer—
my perennial Adirondack hosts
—and friends.

The distance that the dead have gone
Does not at first appear—
Their coming back seems possible
For many an ardent year.

—Emily Dickinson

Contents

Oft in the silence of the night,
When the lonely moon rides high,
When wintry winds are whistling,
And we hear the owl's shrill cry,
In the quiet, dusky chamber,
By the flickering firelight,
Rising up between two sleepers,
Comes a spirit all in white.

— Louisa May Alcott

Introduction

"The woods are lovely, dark and deep," wrote poet-laureate Robert Frost. Hikers contend New York's North Woods are *haunted* as well! Alone in the forest, thoughts of ghostly entities enter the mind and an unnerving presence is perceived. The trekkers feel a shiver as a loon emits its haunting call…

Ghosts *do* inhabit the Adirondack Mountain wilderness—they roam the woodland and the mountain trails.

Philosopher's Camp on the distant shore of Follensby Pond was built by a band of eminent scholars such as Ralph Waldo Emerson, poet James Russell Lowell, Oliver Wendell Holmes and scientist Louis Agassiz. In 1858, Alfred A. Street described this locale as "a haunted place…and many a daring hunter or trapper, laughing at every other peril, trembles if night environs him in its dreaded precincts." Columnist Bill McLaughlin, writing for the *Adirondack Daily Enterprise* speculated: "The illustrious group must have felt the same about it for they later moved the camp to the shores of Ampersand Pond."

Beaver Meadow, on the road from Indian Lake to North Creek, possesses a notorious phantom. Back in the day, the rough and tumble lumberjacks disdained an old, ill-kempt peddler who visited their camp. Perhaps plied with liquid courage, they dragged him out into the night and murdered him. The lumberjacks secreted the peddler, his horse and wagon in a cellar hole and set them ablaze. Legend says the old peddler's wild-looking, white-haired and bearded specter, atop his phantom horse and wagon, bound through Beaver Meadow.

According to reporter Lohr McKinstry, a grove of trees at the bottom of Keene's Spruce Hill marks a former Native American burial mound. In the dead of the night, strange sounds emanate from the suspected gravesite.

Stories of ghostly occupation enshroud the entire region. The Adirondack's physical landscape and its cultural and historic heritage inspire the haunted happenings. The eerie tales seem endless.

Some believe trauma ties a spirit to a place. This could be why Grace Brown's ghost still occupies the environs of Big Moose Lake. The spirits who appear in the following stories were once flesh and blood individuals. Perhaps they all possess an irresistible attachment to the place they frequented in life.

Ghosts are impressions on the ether, or atmosphere. Emotions charge the ether with memories of events. Sensitive people may be able to see these residual energy imprints appearing as spirits. For instance, a location holds the energy of past inhabitants and events and anyone there at the right time can observe a replay of particular actions. This theory can explain why Ellen Hand's spirit still shows up in her Elizabethtown home.

When visiting haunted public places no ghost is going to jump out and send you screaming in terror, although some books, movies and television programs persuade the public to run away in a petrified frenzy when it comes to haunted places. Quite the contrary—spirit encounters can be awe-inspiring and life-changing.

This volume of Adirondack ghost stories presents an array of faithful phantoms. Devoted caretakers carry on at the Glenmore Hotel, Grant Cottage and Wellscroft Lodge. A constant gardener digs in at the Knox Mansion and an ever-present chauffer is on duty at Fort Hudson Health Services. Revenants are revealed from the region's iron mining industry at the Penfield Homestead Museum and Moriah's Town Hall. The Adirondack's long history of hospitality gives rise to a host of spirits at The BrightSide on Raquette and Paul Smith's College.

The accounts in this volume are about subtle presences in Adirondack Park and well-suited for sharing around a crackling fire in the woods or in a comfy lodge. Wherever you decide to curl up, savor the stories of the souls still inhabiting New York's North Country.

The Glenmore – Big Moose Lake

BIG MOOSE LAKE

GLENMORE BAR AND GRILL
& COVEWOOD LODGE

Big Moose Lake is infamous as the setting for Theodore Dreiser's novel *An American Tragedy*.[1] The *true* story concerns Chester Gillette, who was convicted and executed for drowning Grace Brown in the lake's South Bay in 1906. The Academy Award winning film, *A Place in the Sun*, starring Elizabeth Taylor, Shelley Winters and Montgomery Clift, is based on the book.

The murder of Grace Brown continues to gain notoriety as claims of ghost sightings around the lake occur. On July 11, 2006 a wreath-laying ceremony took place on South Bay in observance of the centennial of Brown's death.

Early in the 19th century, Adirondack Railway travelers escaped to the Great North Woods by rail and disembarked at the Big Moose Station. They journeyed to the mountains to flee the daily grind and restore their body, mind and spirit by hunting, fishing, hiking and relaxing.

---

1   Dreiser named the lake where the murder took place, Big Bittern Lake. The author visited Big Moose Lake to add authenticity to his fictional novel.

VIPs lodged at the popular Glenmore
Hotel on Big Moose Lake. Even Vice President
Theodore Roosevelt frequented the hotel
during his hunting forays. On one such trip
Roosevelt learned of President McKinley's
assassination and immediately took the oath of
office as our nation's 26th president.

The original Glenmore Hotel was a grand, four-story Adirondack-style edifice featuring a 200-seat dining room, soda fountain and ice cream parlor. Long before the advent of cell phones, modern radio receiving equipment was available to guests during regular business hours.

In 1950 the Glenmore Hotel burned to the ground.

The building presently housing the Glenmore Bar and Grill served as an annex to the original structure, and at the time of the great fire, operated as the Big Moose Supply Company, the largest store of its kind in the nation during the 1920s. Ultimately, the supply company building underwent renovation and was transformed into the new Glenmore Hotel.

In 1970, Carlton and Marilyn Muller, from Whitesboro, New York, purchased the Glenmore and along with their sons created a family lodging and dining establishment.

Without fail, Bob Muller fields many questions about ghosts at the inn. Often glimpsed is a tall, lanky man dressed in black who moves furtively in and out of the shadows. "Every once in a while you'll see him," said Muller, who lived at the family-owned lodge since he was two-years-old. "He's always been here; I grew up with him, so it's no big deal with me."

Muller feels the specter is James McAllister, a former caretaker who passed suddenly from a heart attack. His mischievous spirit stays behind tinkering with things and making noises. Muller most often spies McAllister's ethereal figure in his peripheral vision.

Intrigued by claims of poltergeist activity, full body apparitions and disembodied voices, the New York State Paranormal Research team investigated the inn. Ten minutes into the search an incorporeal voice said "hey" startling ghost hunters Cano Davy and Marcus Zwierecki. They captured the anomaly on a recorder.

Another electronic voice phenomenon (EVP) recorded that night was an eerie voice from beyond the grave saying "I see you."

McAllister is not the only specter haunting the Glenmore. Another spirit who frequents the environs of the lakeside restaurant is Grace Brown.

Social climber Chester Gillette murdered 19-year-old Grace Brown on July 11, 1906. Pregnant with his child Gillette lured the naïve farm girl to the remote wilderness. He had a hidden agenda—she held hopes of getting married. The night before Grace ended up on the bottom of the lake, she and Gillette lodged at the Glenmore.

Initially Gillette denied knowing the girl but justice prevailed. Ultimately, he was convicted and executed by electric chair.

Unsolved Mysteries told the story of the young woman's murder and subsequent sightings of Grace Brown's ghost in a television episode that premiered in 1996.[2] When the

---

2   The author's ghost sighting and more information about the *Unsolved Mysteries* production appear in *Adirondack Ghosts* (Black Cat Press, 2000).

show's producer consulted with a couple at
the Glenmore Hotel regarding ghost sightings,
they responded that one night as they dined,
her ephemeral form floated outside the large
picture window overlooking the lake. The pair
declined to appear on the program.

The July 16, 1909 edition of *The Plattsburgh
Sentinel* reported the sighting of a little skiff on
the placid waters where Grace met her death.
The phantom rowboat resembled the one rented
by the couple on that fateful day and contained
a young man and woman. The mysterious
watercraft appeared on moonlit nights.

At nearby **Covewood Lodge**, Jim Dunning
of Ashburn, Virginia received a startling
surprise at dawn one sunny August day in
2000.

His morning ritual included a swim from
the lakeside dock out to the floating dock.
Upon returning to the lakeside dock around
6:00 A. M. he discovered a small, wet footprint

on one of the steps leading out of the water onto the dock. Only a single footprint—nothing before it or nothing after it. Additionally, Jim remained within sight of the dock during his entire swim. There was no way he would have missed seeing another person.

He shared his story via e-mail:

We stay in Lakeside every year, and when the kids were younger they got a big kick out of watching the UNSOLVED MYSTERIES episode about Grace Brown because the reenactment used our cabin. Made it a bit creepier. The first time we did that I think all of them ended up sharing the living room all night because they were so freaked out.

I have no idea where the footprint came from. However, I do know it was very unlikely there was anyone else on that dock with me that morning. Every summer we've stayed at Covewood (18 so far) I've never missed my morning swim across the Outlet. It's always between 5:45 and 6:45, and although I'm swimming away from the Lakeside dock for half of it, I'm constantly turning around in the water and watching the morning activity (which rarely includes people).

I've always said I would have seen anyone on the dock that morning. And the other thing that puzzled me was there was only a single footprint. Still wet, on the top rise of the ladder coming out of the water, but no other signs of water neither on the other couple risers above water nor on the dock. I have no way of knowing who actually left the footprint; I just know it was very strange I never saw nor heard her or him.

Needless to say, the mysterious footprint caused the hairs on the back of Jim's neck to rise. He continued to share humorous "haunting" stories I feel bear telling:

For a number of years now we've taken it upon ourselves to "add" to the Grace Brown mystery by presenting a haunting every summer. It's taken many forms with some interesting results.

9

Covewood Lodge

One of the more raucous shows had the docks full of numerous families at about 10 P. M. involved a small weather balloon, helium, and glow sticks to create a glowing object floating over the water in front of the Lodge.

The first year we did something a bit sticky, however. We surreptitiously strung a fish line pulley contraption across the Outlet from the base of Buzz Point right before sundown. Of course, we were praying no one returned a motor boat any time soon. The other end was attached to a white garbage bag with glow sticks in it; it was hidden in the bushes near the path leading from the Children's Beach to the Lodge. Once it was dark we waited on Buzz Point until we saw flashlights bobbing through the woods heading for the beach. Just as they reached the hidden bag we yanked the 100 feet of line and the ghost popped straight up and started jerking its way across the water, followed by teenage girls' screams!

The two 40-year-old "boys" behind this prank panicked at this unexpected level of commotion and pulled Grace across the water as quickly as possible, spurred on by the shouting mob of curious teens racing for the footbridge.

Perhaps Grace left her footprint behind for Jim as a stamp of approval in support of keeping her memory and spirit alive... so to speak.

CHESTERTOWN

CHESTER HOUSE

Situated between the Hudson and Schroon Rivers, Chestertown was originally known as "the Crossroads." The town's place in history includes its role as a stop on the illegal trade route for alcohol during the prohibition era.

In the 1800s, the economy depended on timbering and natural resources, but by the 20th century, the Adirondacks bustled as a tourist destination. Chestertown's sparkling lakes drew generations of families who still consider the village a favored journey's end.

The Chester House formerly stood on the corner of Main Street and Theriot Avenue. The 100-plus room lodge loomed over the small hamlet. Built in the mid-19th century, during Chestertown's boom years, the guesthouse became the thriving town's center.

For over a century guests enjoyed the hotel's amenities and townspeople often whispered about a ghost who flitted about its upper floors.

The Chester House ghost supposedly was the spirit of a New York City actor who committed suicide by hanging himself from the attic rafters. A ghoulish rumor attached to the legend was the noose decapitated the man. For that reason, his *headless* phantom haunted the place.

CROWN POINT

PENFIELD HOMESTEAD
MUSEUM

Located in historic Ironville in the Town of Crown Point, the Penfield Homestead Museum is dedicated to preserving the history of the North Country's ironworking industry during the 19th century. This hamlet is considered the "Birthplace of the Electric Age" because the site is the first industrial setting where electricity was utilized in the United States.

The region prompted modern progress and supported Union efforts during the Civil War. Iron ore mined in the nearby hamlet of Hammondville was separated in Ironville and shipped by railroad to Lake Champlain where it was used in many applications including the Civil War ironclad *U.S.S. Monitor*.

U. S. S. Monitor

The Penfield Foundation preserves and protects the historic landscape and hamlet as well as Crown Point Iron Company history in addition to the legacy of the Penfield Family. For ten years I sensed a haunting presence in the Penfield home and Crown Point historian, Joan Hunsdon, recently validated my feelings.

All sorts of noises plague the house as do furtive black shadows. In the dining room, tea cups are set on the table display yet invariably one is found moved to the side by the fireplace. Strangely enough, a chair also finds its way closer to the fireplace. Mrs. Hunsdon feels the spirit rearranging the furnishings is Miss Annie.

Miss Annie was an unmarried woman and the last Penfield to occupy, I mean *still* occupy, the house. A volunteer once felt shoved by unseen hands outside what used to be Miss Annie's bedroom.

Lights are found on in the home when they were definitely turned off. This oddity particularly occurs in the office. The workplace also often feels icy cold even on the warmest of summer days. Adding to the intrigue is a former caretaker heard a heated argument ensuing in the space. Men's loud voices were discerned yet what they actually said was unintelligible. Phantom fists banging the table also mystified the curator.

A local ghost hunting group headed by the Thatcher family investigated the property. No paranormal probe is complete without an arsenal of detection equipment. Certain devices failed to work at Penfield but when removed from the building they functioned fine. Mrs. Hunsdon felt Miss Annie didn't like all the new fangled gadgets. Hey, she doesn't even like her teacup moved. It's hard to imagine what an earthbound existence must be like for those souls who stay behind. Imagine living in your house, not knowing you're dead and having complete strangers invade your property...

The investigation turned up little—in fact, they found the place to be *abnormally* quiet!

Explore the wonders of living during this era by visiting 703 Creek Road in historic Ironville but try not to get into any "spirited" arguments.

DANNEMORA

CLINTON PRISON
POWER PLANT

"**M**ark my words," insisted the old timers, "that place'll be haunted!" Sure enough their prediction came true.

The Clinton State Correctional Facility in Dannemora is sometimes called "Siberia." The cold climate and the isolated area is the setting for the largest maximum security facility and the third oldest prison in New York State.

Established in 1845 after a period of steady rising crime, the prison began as a tiny outpost with a few small buildings surrounded by a wooden stockade fence. Originally the prisoners worked in local mines in both Dannemora and nearby Lyon Mountain. Many prisoners were cured of tuberculosis due in part to the region's fresh, balsam-scented air; this led to the importation of prisoners with this disease from other lock-ups.

In 1929, the Clinton prison witnessed a riot which, coupled with unrest in other facilities that year, led to prison reform in New York State. Totally renovated by 1931, the rebuilding included cellblocks, schools, service buildings, and supporting structures. Authorities hoped the huge, modern facility would alleviate any more trouble.

During the expansion a new power plant was constructed over the site of a former graveyard. Surprisingly, the cemetery movers unearthed an iron coffin with a glass lid.

Cast-iron coffins are rare and were primarily in use between 1850 and 1870. Such caskets cost $50 to $100 while an average person's casket ran $2 to $3. Cast-iron coffins were watertight and ensured preservation of the body and clothing. The iron itself helped preserve the remains.

The exhumed coffin contained the preserved body of a 17-year-old boy. "Even the blond hair of the boy was perfectly combed and parted," according to the *Chateaugay Record*. A long-time resident said the young man died over seventy years earlier during the smallpox epidemic.

At the time, superstition held sway; disinterring a body would bring bad luck— *or worse*. The town elders' prediction came to pass...

Night watchmen were so spooked by mysterious sounds that several left their jobs in quick succession giving vague reasons for their departure. The only remaining guard said his comrades left because the place was haunted. He carried firearms to work for protection as he suspected a more earthly explanation for the strange noises.

One night he routinely investigated the sounds outside and in doing so crossed over a deep, plank-covered pit. Returning by the same route he almost fell to his death down the dangerous ditch because someone removed the planking.

"The next day a new watchman was being sought," summed up the *Chateaugay Record* reporter.

ELIZABETHTOWN

ADIRONDACK HISTORY
CENTER MUSEUM

Henry Deletnack De Bosnys was the last man to hang in New York's Essex County. His skull is on display at Elizabethtown's Adirondack History Center Museum at 7590 Court Street. Is it any wonder his restless spirit still lurks about the former high school building?

Hanged April 27, 1883 at the old county courthouse De Bosnys was convicted of murdering his wife and sentenced to death. After the hanging, people speculated the mysterious stranger arrived in Elizabethtown with an agenda. He wooed the pretty widow in order to claim her fortune as his own. This motive precipitated her demise on a hiking trail where DeBosnys brutally stabbed and shot her to death. Witnesses observed him secreting her body under leaves at the side of a dirt road. He adamantly denied his guilt but a jury took only ten minutes to convict him.

The supposed solider of fortune claimed he traveled the world. He bragged about serving in the U.S. 7th Cavalry under Colonel George Armstrong Custer at the Battle of Little

Bighorn. None of his self-important stories were ever proven in fact.

This may not have been his first crime, says the Museum Educator Lindsay Pontius. He allegedly killed a laundress before relocating to the North Country.

Museum Director Margaret Gibbs said one of the museum's summer interns reported seeing De Bosnys' ghost. Ironically, the student later learned one of her ancestors officially sanctioned the criminal's hanging. Although his conviction was justified, did the brazen killer appear to the young woman to display disdain for her forebear who supported his guilty verdict? No one other than the young woman ever spotted his wraith. Perhaps the intern possesses a special psychic link.

It gets stranger. Staffers found a newspaper clipping about the murder case in the copy machine. No one put it there—no one *living*, that is. The document was kept under wraps for years because there was no reason to retrieve it. As museum workers pondered the mysterious event the lights went out.

Before his execution, De Bosnys sold his body to a local physician for $15 in exchange for a suit to wear on his execution day. Ever the narcissist, he wanted to impress his audience until his dying day. The doctor dissected the man's body and donated the skeletal remains to a local school. All that remains of De Bosnys today is the skull preserved in the museum—along with the spirit of a shameless psychopath.

THE DEER'S HEAD INN

In 1808 the Simmond's Cottage was built to accommodate North Woods' travelers. When the building sustained damage during a fire 20 years later, what remained of the structure was moved to the Deer's Head Inn's present location on Court Street opposite the Essex County Courthouse. Rebuilt as the Mansion House, the hostelry prospered for 40 years and then became the Deer's Head Inn.

The lodging supported troops during the War of 1812 when Army personnel commandeered the building for use as a hospital. Not only did the structure shelter those injured in the Battle of Plattsburgh, for a time, the structure also served as a school.

During Prohibition the owner of the Deer's Head concealed his entire liquor inventory under the porch. The safely ensconced cache was accessed through a hidden door by using a long pole. When the porch underwent repair in 1991, a number of bottles turned up. They remain on display above the bar.

Two U.S. Presidents lodged at the Deer's Head Inn. The signatures of Grover Cleveland and Benjamin Harrison appear in the inn's register. Another notable guest was abolitionist John Brown's widow who spent the night while her husband's body lay in state at the nearby courthouse.

Joanne Baldwin, one of the inn's owners, doesn't spend a lot of time tracking down the paranormal at her restaurant but she feels the place accommodates at least one ghost.

She hears the spirit's disembodied footsteps upstairs. Might the elusive entity be a deceased soldier from the 1800s? Or a long-term guest who refuses to leave? Even a few diners observed the spirit but second-guessed their visions.

Joanne told of unexplainable events in the restaurant. *Every* day it seems something inexplicable occurs. For instance, crumbs will be swept off the table and upon returning with the place settings the crumbs are back! Or a glass of wine will be poured, the bottle replaced behind the bar and when the bartender goes to serve the glass of wine it's not there! It's happenings such as these that gives one pause…

Joanne spoke about a server who once worked there who was not exactly a "team player." The worker only looked out for herself and exuded a strange vibe. The restaurant's spirit seemed to take exception to her as well because the young woman inexplicably provoked the phantom's ire. For instance, on occasion the swinging door to the kitchen would not budge for her. It wouldn't open making it near impossible for her to perform her job.

Catering to guests for over 200 years, the Deer's Head Inn endures as "the Adirondack's Oldest Inn." An ancient structure with a human history—the perfect combination for a haunted setting.

HAND HOUSE

In 1849, Judge Augustus C. Hand commissioned the five-bedroom home on River Street. Many original artifacts still inhabit the house along with the spirit of a young woman.

The Bruce L. Crary Foundation grants scholarships to area students and since 1979 has owned the historic home. Hannelore Kissam served as the foundation's Executive Director for 23 years and possesses first hand knowledge of inexplicable incidents in the house. "Little things happen all the time," she proclaimed.

Hanne went on to say that when the Franciscan Friars stayed there one of the young men awoke to the sound of footsteps outside his bedroom door. Then he heard the door open, felt someone sit on his bed and then lay on top of him! Terrified, he endured the heavy pressure for several minutes until the invisible figure got up, opened the door and walked down the hall. Oddly, his roommate in the adjacent twin bed slept like a log. Petrified, he waited until daybreak then rushed down the street to the church rectory in order to discuss the incident with the priest. He never entered the house again.

There was a point in Hanna's life when she spent six weeks recovering from surgery in the house. She and her 11-year-old son stayed on the second floor. Hanna couldn't afford to miss work and she enjoyed her job.

One particular night, at about 1:00 A. M., as her son slept in the next room, she heard a sound out in the hall. Then the doorknob to her room turned. Hanne thought it was her son getting up when she heard more noises out in the hallway. She always felt comfortable in the house so she got up, opened the door and saw someone at the end of the hall walking toward the servants' quarters. She observed a slight, dark-haired woman going *through* the door. The strange thing that struck Hanne at the time was there was no reflection of the woman in the large mirror.

During the course of her workday, Hanne would perceive the harmless presence and described the spirit as someone lost. She explained the subtle encounter as a whiff of human body odor masked with a flowery perfume. It wasn't offensive, she said, more of a body smell than we are accustomed to people emitting today. Most times she noticed this scent near the dining room where a portrait of Ellen Hand now hangs. The petite, brunette was Judge Hand's daughter who passed away shortly after her marriage.

STONELEIGH BED & BREAKFAST

Castle-like Stoneleigh B & B nestles cozily in the woods off River Street. The soothing sound of Barton Brook trickles out front creating a tranquil ambiance guests enjoy. The inn is a peaceful get-a-way where six inviting fireplaces entice guests to cuddle up with a good (ghost!) book. Although it looks like it could be haunted, I'd say it's purr-fectly spirited.

Judge Francis Smith and his wife, Julia Scott Smith, bought Stoneleigh in 1884. The distinctive dwelling was inspired by H. H. Richardson's architectural style and modeled after elegant European castles. The Smiths adopted a daughter, Louise. After her parents' death, she resided in the stone home with her cats until she passed away in the 1950s.

The house served as a nursing home for a time. The renovations required to transform the building into a care center covered up, and even destroyed, some of the structure's special architectural appointments.

When Ronald and Rosemary Remington, and their daughter Rebecca, first looked at the place as a potential home in 1969 the structure sat vacant and was coated with a thick layer of dust. Ronald had reservations about buying the place but Rosemary regarded the house as a diamond in the rough.

A big, gray tabby cat sat in the library doorway as if to welcome the family. Ronald went to fetch the creature but he scooted away. Ronald pursued the errant pet but the feline was nowhere to be found. Ronald thought it odd the cat's scamper left no trace on the dusty

STONELEIGH

BED & BREAKFAST

floor... The house sat empty for years so how did the tabby even get in the house?

Busy refurbishing their new abode, the cat's appearance upstairs confounded the couple. Who owned this beast? None of the neighbors knew. Ronald searched the house high and low but never found the elusive kitty.

Within a few years the Remingtons returned the place to its original splendor. Ronald noticed the big, grey tomcat outside in the driveway as if smiling his approval.

In 1987, Rosemary decided to open the house as a bed and breakfast inn. On occasion a guest will ask if she owns a cat. Rosemary shakes her head and smiles knowing what will follow. Some visitors claim to feel a cat jump on the bed and walk across their pillow during the night. Invariably the guest finds it comforting because they've left their own pet behind. Rosemary's hospitality and Stoneleigh's phantom cat makes them feel right at home.

FORT EDWARD

FORT HUDSON
HEALTH SERVICES

The Howland Estate consisted of three large family homes and encompassed all of what today is the Fort Hudson Health Services property.

The Howland residences were owned by Ethel (nee Howland) and her husband J. E. Goodfellow who became Village President in 1888. He held an interest in Fort Edward Machine Works, and two local paint and pulp companies. The Goodfellows bore one daughter.

Lansing M. Howland and his wife built their house in 1892. The residence was often referred to as "Mr. Howland's Gingerbread House" or "The Towers." Howland was an officer of Howland Paper Company in Sandy Hill (today's Hudson Falls).

Mrs. Howland belonged to the New York State Woman Suffrage Party and often held fundraising functions in her home. Lansing Howland died suddenly in his 50s.

The Howlands were one of the first people to own a car and they employed a chauffeur who lived in a small cottage on the property.

Rumor has it that the Goodfellow's daughter eloped with Howland's chauffeur.

The main drive to the house is the same driveway that leads to the nursing home circle. Lansing Howland's house was situated approximately where the traffic circle and lobby area are today.

Enos Howland and his wife, (Lansing's parents), owned the third house.

Given the number of people who inhabited the site it's tricky identifying those haunting the property.

Several employees at the health center have observed a male apparition formally dressed in black roaming the halls. Could this vision be the chauffer? On the other hand, Lansing G. Howland died prematurely. Fort Edward historian Paul McCarty provided the historical background of the property. He reminded me that since Lansing was a successful businessman, a Chief Executive Officer, if you will, he would always be properly dressed. Perhaps Lansing is the specter who wanders from room to room and slowly fades away.

Mrs. Howland's fortune suffered in the stock market crash of 1929. Her economic downturn necessitated the sale of her grand home. She ultimately took up residence in the Greenwich Home for Aged Women.

Residents and staff members at the health center also witness a woman in a white night gown peering out a second floor window. Maybe this phantom is Mrs. Howland's spirit. Possibly she stays behind, choosing to eternally dwell in the comfort of her long-ago, home.

HUDSON FALLS

THE HERALD BUILDING

The Village Booksmith is a Hudson Falls landmark since 1976. Two buildings comprise the popular bookshop owned by Cliff and Jean Bruce. The smaller corner building once housed *The Herald*, a Sandy Hill[3] newspaper. The upper floor served as the editor's residence.

Bruce stated the structure's ceilings are of a normal height except in the back where they are higher. He suspects the height is raised in order to accommodate the huge printing presses once housed in the building. Before the Bruces possessed the second, smaller building the then owner rented the upper floor.

Hudson Falls' resident Robyn Brown experienced a ghostly encounter in 1977 at the Village Booksmith's corner building. Her friend Patty lived in the upstairs apartment. For awhile Patty complained to Robyn about the towels in the bathroom that kept ending up on the floor no matter how many times she picked them up.

One night the friends arrived at Patty's

3   The town of Hudson Falls was known as Sandy Hill until the turn of the 20th century.

(Print of "The Herald" building courtesy of Cliff and Jean Bruce.)

apartment laden with groceries. The pair
walked toward the kitchen and stopped dead
in their tracks. A strange man, who looked
as startled as they were, stood in the kitchen
doorway and stared at the two women. The
balding man wore a white shirt with rolled
up sleeves and suspenders. He disappeared
as soon as he appeared. Patty later learned a
printer once lived there.

In 35 years as proprietors, Bruce and Jean
never experienced the paranormal at the
bookshop. Given the site's history as a print shop
and newspaper office the specter's appearance
makes sense to the women. Nevertheless, it's an
experience they'll never forget.

THE HUDSON FALLS
FREE LIBRARY

Concerned citizens founded the Hudson Falls
Free Library in 1910. The trustees appointed
Genevieve Clark as librarian. Miss Clark, a
junior high school English teacher established
the library in her home. For $750.00 *per year*,
the librarian offered her services six afternoons
and evenings a week.

When Miss Clark retired in 1928 Esther
Sherman took over the vacated position.
She retired in 1973. That same year Marie L.
Gandron became the present library director.

Built in 1916, the classic library building at
220 Main Street harbors more than books but
surprisingly, Ms. Gandron does not feel that
those who linger at the library are her long-
term predecessors.

Strange noises and unexplained activities
are common occurrences. For instance, books
that are held in reserve are stored in a special
drawer. When they need to be retrieved

they're no where to be found. A short time later the on-duty librarian will return to the drawer and the reserved books have magically re-appeared. Other items go missing only to show up later exactly where they were supposed to be in the first place.

At times, Marie arrived at work and found *every* light on in the place. She can understand leaving one or two lights ablaze but every light burning is unexplainable.

The head librarian usually breaks for dinner around 5:30 P. M. and heads downstairs for some privacy. The first time she heard the footsteps overhead she thought she forgot to lock the library entrance door or that she locked someone in the building. This was not the case. The mysterious footsteps resound over and over—everyone who works there hears them.

On at least one occasion a staffer could not open the door even though it wasn't locked. No matter how hard she tried the door wouldn't budge.

More than one person observed the

impression of a man's face on the fireplace. Sometimes his image is scowling yet at other times he smiles. A psychic medium channeled the man's spirit. He claimed to be a former patron who donated $15.00, according to historic records. Due to his "generosity," he feels entitled to linger at the place. His sullen face appears to show his displeasure when his favorite chair by the fireplace is moved.

The worker who delivers the books obtained through inter-library loan is of Pakistan descent. One day he approached Marie looking as white as a sheet. He conveyed to the librarian that a woman was in the building who "didn't belong" (implying she was not of this world). He described the female apparition as dressed in a long skirt and "boots," meaning high-button shoes, according to Marie. The specter's hairstyle was an upsweep in typical Victorian fashion. Astoundingly, her phantom form vanished into the stacks, he said.

A psychic contacted the spectral interloper and Marie conveyed that her name is "Joanna," a woman who once lived in a house next door that was razed to make way for the municipal building. Joanna's spirit said she appeared to the man because *he* "didn't belong" there because of his dark skin, revealing her 19th century attitude.

The Adirondack Paranormal Society investigated the building and spent the night searching for evidence. Their high-tech ghost hunting equipment registered readings off the chart clearly indicating paranormal activity.

The library celebrates its 100th anniversary next year, and Marie feels proud to be part of its (haunted) history.

(Photo courtesy of Anthony Leiker).

INLET

GREAT CAMP ALBEDOR

Wealthy publisher Colonel Edward Simmons built the historic Albedor Great Camp in 1928. The successful businessman chaired several companies and served on the boards of many others. President Calvin Coolidge named him a delegate to an international railway conference in London. The Colonel was also a family man and christened his massive Fourth Lake retreat "Albedor" after his three daughters—Aline, Betty and Doris.

Located on 16 acres with 900 feet of waterfront, the 17,000 square foot home offers spectacular views from every room. The property boasts 14 bedrooms, 12 ½ baths, two-story boathouse with a 2000 square foot play room, basketball, tennis and volleyball courts and a children's playground. The living room of the private home, which is available to rent, is dominated by a 10-foot wide fireplace hand hammered from one giant boulder native to the property.

Adding to the wealth, the wonderful house also possesses a spirit from the past.

The long-standing ghost story associated

with the great camp involves a worker who entered a second floor room and observed a young girl playing. He didn't think her presence unusual and assumed one of the other workmen brought his child to the job. When he asked the men about her no one knew who he was talking about. He returned to the girl but she was no longer there.

It is generally believed that the vision was the spirit of the Simmons' oldest daughter Aline who was killed when she was an adult. She was struck by a car in Orlando, Florida and killed instantly on November 22, 1963, the day of the Kennedy assassination.

Other people who worked at the great camp fled the house and wouldn't return. It's hard to imagine a spectral child could scare adults out of their wits.

The camp was bequeathed to a Brooklyn orphanage when Mrs. Simmons died and some believe the ghost belongs to one of the orphans. In truth, the Brooklyn home immediately sold the Albedor to a private owner.

An informant from Raquette Lake, who wishes to remain anonymous, conveyed that a friend who worked there gave her a tour of the *empty* house. They came up from the wine cellar and upon entering the living room a couple of the windows looked damp with condensation (vaporous steam, mist and fog are often associated with paranormal activity). The Raquette Lake woman immediately noticed child-size handprints on the misty glass as if an ethereal youngster stood looking out the window.

Owner Anthony Leiker hasn't personally encountered any spirits at his Great Camp but he appreciates the haunted heritage of his historic home.

JOHNSTOWN

KNOX MANSION

The Knox Mansion is a historical house built in 1889 by gelatin magnate Charles Knox. Knox produced the world's first pre-granulated gelatin in the late 19th century. The revolutionary product significantly impacted modern cooking. Today the brand is owned by Kraft Foods but for several decades was produced in Johnstown.

Charles' wife, Rose, wrote recipe booklets to promote the versatile use of this product in molded desserts, salads and cold soups. Over a million were distributed every year. Knox allotted his wife a weekly stipend and permitted Rose to do anything with the money as she pleased.

When her husband passed away in 1908, Rose took over the business. Immediately, she closed the back door of the factory formerly used by the women—men entered by the front door. She believed in male and female equality; no longer would the sexes use separate doors. When she overheard one of her husband's top executives say he would not work for a woman, she asked for his resignation.

The progressive woman went on to establish a five day work week and gave her workers two weeks of paid vacation, an unprecedented benefit. Remarkably, under Mrs. Knox's leadership, the gelatin company survived the Great Depression without having to release any of its workers.

It's no surprise that many feel the spirit of this strong pioneering woman still pervades her earthly abode.

The Knox mansion is a national historic landmark and is currently owned by Marty Quinn who runs the house as a bed and breakfast inn and museum. The mansion boasts 42 rooms, an elevator, a grand staircase and a solid lava ash fireplace imported from an Italian castle. The residence retains mysterious cubicles as well. In the billiard room a small panel is secreted in a bookcase—most likely used for concealing valuables. A tiny, three-foot high portal leads to a hideaway off an attic bedroom.

Throughout Quinn's 15 years as owner all manner of paranormal activity has occurred in the house. Inexplicably, lights and the television turn on and off. Curiously, fragile items are found broken and eerie footsteps resound. The owner said blankets are pulled off the bed during the night. Does Rose Knox have a hand in these anomalies? She may be a frustrated spirit seeking to make her presence known.

Even Quinn's two daughters experienced unexplainable phenomena—Sara felt a presence walk right through her and Amy heard voices and sensed being watched.

Overnight guests shared dozens of supernatural stories experienced during their stay. They claim to hear the din of disembodied voices. They endured cold spots, sighted ghosts and discerned a phantom pianist. Some say an unseen presence touched them. One visitor observed a male specter carrying what looked like a doctor's satchel. This entity may be the spirit of a previous owner who was a physician and allegedly died by his own hand.

A few detect a ghostly figure in the basement; he is believed to be the former gardener. Kids, in particular, perceive the long-gone gardener who in life especially delighted in children's company.

Furthermore, spectral children are heard in the mansion on occasion when none are present. A lot of people say they've seen a little girl's apparition.

Adding to the creep factor is Charles and Rose Knox considered the number 13 auspicious and even designed their home with their lucky number in mind. For instance, there are thirteen tiles in the fireplace and thirteen steps on the grand staircase.

On Halloween nights Quinn covers the house with cobwebs, scary paintings and sinister statues. He conducts a haunted house tour complete with costumed actors. Over 1,000 people show up to explore the decked-out manse and enjoy some good old-fashioned scares.

If you spot a ghost in the window on October 31st it may not be a decoration…

KEENE VALLEY

AUSABLE INN

Martha Allen of the *Lake Placid News* reported that 30 years ago when the hostelry operated as the Spread Eagle a couple lived in the main bedroom. They experienced lights, television and radio repeatedly coming on in the middle of the night without explanation.

Guests at the Ausable Inn reported footsteps outside their room running up and down the hall when no one was there. They complained the water in the shower turned on and off for no reason. Some were even locked out, or in, their rooms.

Baseball caps mysteriously flying from the shelves left employees scratching their heads in wonder...

In her article, "Is Keene Valley Haunted?" Martha wrote that as she sat at the bar chatting with a friend she felt an invisible someone brush by her. She intuitively discerned a young man passing in the direction of the front door but when she looked up no one was there. Although she didn't mention the sensation

to her companion, a split second afterward
Martha's friend glanced around as if to see
who walked behind her. Both women might
have thought they imagined the phenomenon
had they not validated each other's experience.

LAKE PLACID

JOHN BROWN FARM

Lake Placid is the eternal resting place of abolitionist John Brown. This historic property commemorates the man who fought against slavery and thereby created one of the most enduring legends in the nation's history.

In 1849, John Brown moved from Springfield, Massachusetts, where he was an active conductor on the Underground Railroad. Wealthy businessman Gerrit Smith gave parcels of land in upstate New York to free African Americans. Purchasing a lot from Smith, Brown moved his family to the wilderness area where for ten years he guided and taught the struggling families who set out to develop their own farms.

John Brown moved to Kansas in 1855 where two of his sons led armed revolts proslavery forces. He returned to his upstate farm six times to visit his wife and some of his children.

On the night of October 16, 1859, John Brown and his followers raided the U. S. Arsenal at Harper's Ferry to capture firearms for use in a forceful campaign to liberate the slaves. Brown was arrested and imprisoned at Charlestown, Virginia, where he was tried and hanged on December 2, 1859. His mortal remains were returned to his Adirondack home and interred in the front yard.

Soon after Brown's death his homestead became a pilgrimage site for free African Americans and white abolitionists.

Ultimately the Lake Placid community declined due to its remote location and harsh climate. In due course, Brown's family moved to California at the onset of the Civil War.

In 1870, the John Brown Association purchased the farm and gravesite. The State of New York received ownership in 1896.

Linda Roy is the historic site's interpreter and has led tours of John Brown's farmhouse for 23 summer seasons. While researching the location's history, Linda discovered her great, great grandmother, Elizabeth Reed, also worked at the Brown farm during the summer months decades earlier. Perhaps this family connection is why Linda feels so attached to the place. Her intuitive gifts add an especially extraordinary dimension to her relationship to the location.

The Hughes family farmed the land a hundred years ago. Their son, Billy, died from a lightning strike while plowing a field. Linda discerned his presence during her fourth year at the farm. The interpreter spotted Billy at the foot of the cellar stairs looking up at her. His form glowed with a reddish aura (the after effect of being struck by lightning?). On another occasion she spied his silhouette standing in the root cellar. Some visitors sight Billy's phantom form standing at the living room window.

John Brown's daughter-in-law Martha passed away shortly after giving birth to daughter Olive. The child passed on shortly thereafter. When downstairs, Linda often discerns the movement of the rocking chair overhead. The docent feels the sound is the devoted mother's spirit carrying on her maternal duties.

The John Brown Farm is slightly off the beaten track on John Brown Road, south of the intersection with Old Military Road in Lake Placid. The tranquil enclave evokes a time gone by but not for the spirits still lingering there.

GOODSELL HOUSE

The Town of Webb Historical Society is housed in an 1899 Victorian home built by George Goodsell, a local stagecoach driver and hotel builder. Goodsell's son also resided there and when he passed away in 1994, at age 100, he bequeathed the home to the historical society.

The Goodsell House is listed on the New York State and National Historic Registers and every year the museum mounts an Adirondack-themed exhibit.

The residence faithfully retains its original appearance. Visitors sense the stirrings of a by-gone era walking past the venerable, giant oaks and onto the open front porch. The home's focal point is an elegant oak staircase arching up to the second floor. Wainscoting and vintage lighting add to the classic atmosphere. Goodsell's desk, safe, portrait and other family furnishings are on display.

Joyce Haag is the former director of the Town of Webb Historical Association. During her tenure she experienced some paranormal incidents at the house. After locking up for the night she'd slowly drive away and give the place a backward glance. On more than one occasion she observed a surreptitious hand pull the curtain as if whoever was inside stood and watched Joyce leave for the day.

Another common occurrence was the disembodied footsteps heard on the second floor. Joyce perceived the footfalls when all was quiet and no one else was present in the house. Nevertheless, she called out to the invisible visitor but never received an answer.

Tapping into their intuition, the general consensus among those who sense the presence is that the spirit is Tina, George Goodsell's daughter.

(Paul Smith's Hotel photo courtesy of Library of Congress).

PAUL SMITH'S

PAUL SMITHS COLLEGE

Paul Smith's College is named for a man whose famous resort on Lower St. Regis Lake was synonymous with Adirondack hospitality. During the late 19th and early 20th centuries many of the rich and famous, including presidents and statesmen, gathered to enjoy the mountain wilderness and comfortable accommodations provided by Apollos A. (Paul) Smith and his wife, Lydia.

Born in Milton, Vermont in 1825, when Paul first ventured to the Adirondack Mountains he envisioned endless opportunities. In 1858, he purchased 50 acres on Lower St. Regis Lake and established his namesake hotel—the site where Paul Smith's College now stands. The entrepreneur bequeathed his estate for the establishment of a learning institution in his name.

The property's long history of habitation lends itself to the mysterious; tragic events also helped to influence its haunted history.

According to alumna Stephen Cobb, a campus safety officer working the graveyard shift was afforded a glimpse of the historical past. After completing his rounds, the guard took his dinner break around 3:00 A. M. and dozed off in his patrol car. Startled awake by the sound of someone tapping on the vehicle's window, he alertly snapped to and opened the steamed-up window. An unfamiliar man asked the security officer if he needed assistance. He assured the stranger he was fine. That was a true statement until the officer peered through the blurred windshield and caught a glimpse of a vintage coach hitched to a team of horses. The guard's brain felt as foggy as his windows... He soon realized the man who checked on him wore an old-fashioned, double-breasted coat, similar to the uniforms worn by the stagecoach drivers from the old hotel. The antique vehicle vanished before the stunned officer's eyes.

A tragic event occurred during construction of the school's gymnasium. An electrician fell to his death from the scaffolding while installing ceiling lights. Many feel his spirit is responsible for the strange light show occurring late in the night in the secured building.

The phantom electrician orchestrates the lights to turn on and off in a wave sequence. Numerous inspectors allege the phenomenon is *impossible* because the lights are wired to turn on as banks of lights not individual rows.

The Phelps Smith Administration Building possesses the ghost of a former safety officer who apparently is still on watch. The story goes that one bitter night as the officer drove on curvy Route 30 the officer ran off the road and died. The officer took pride in his work and his spirit continues to show up for work. He carried his orderly obsession to the Other Side because on some winter mornings, when road conditions are similar to that fateful day, the staff will arrive to find pamphlets lining the stairs from the basement to the second floor, one per step, in a perfect line.

Lydia Martin Smith watches over her

namesake building. Old-fashioned Lydia, with her dyed-in-the-wool values, apparently disapproves of young men living in the same building as unmarried women. Her spirit occasionally perplexes the male students living in the dorm. One student awoke to find an old woman sitting in his rocking chair watching him sleep. "Hello, Lydia," he said and watched her apparition fade away.

(Photo courtesy of Dr. Jimmy Emerson).

PORT HENRY

MORIAH TOWN HALL

Moriah Town Hall is a French Second Empire structure built in 1875 and the former Witherbee Sherman Company headquarters. The iron company's office building, one of three historic buildings on Park Place, now houses the town's government offices.

Historically, the iron-mining industry played a central role in Moriah's development so it's no surprise a revenant from that era stays behind.

Moriah Town Supervisor, Thomas R. Scozzafava took time out from his busy schedule to speak with me about the odd goings-on in the building.

He said the third floor is the most active. The space is alive with at least one diligent worker from an earlier age. The floor is unused but Tom describes it as an immense open area with large ceiling lights that once illuminated drafting and planning tables utilized when the building housed Republic Steel.

Staffers working at night in the building, including Tom, report hearing phantom workers toiling on the closed-off third floor. Barbara Brassard, now the Ticonderoga Chamber of Commerce Executive Director, was employed at the town hall for 13 years. She said she never believed in ghosts until she worked at the old building. She wouldn't dream of going there alone at night. She too claimed echoes of the past resounded on the third floor—Barbara swore something lived upstairs.

Barbara maintained "things were not quite right" there. Small items would go missing. For instance, she always kept a toothbrush and paste at work and both went missing. What co-worker would steal someone's toothbrush? Unexplainably, files disappeared. When unusual incidents such as these occur over and over the culprit could be a poltergeist. A poltergeist is an earthbound spirit who is frustrated that no one seems to notice them. As a result they try to attract attention by making noises, moving or stealing things.

The *Press Republican* printed a story about a male figure who peered out a third-story window. The specter, who they dubbed Fred, is thought to be someone who perished there when the mining company owned the brick building, said the reporter.

LEE HOUSE APARTMENTS

Once the largest hotel in Port Henry, the Italianate style Lee House on South Main Street opened across from the village green in 1877. The hostelry boasted 50 guest rooms and introduced one of the first Otis elevators. Saved from demolition, the building underwent renovation and today serves as housing for senior citizens.

If you stroll down the upstairs hallway at the right time time, you might glimpse a ghost. Some say they've spotted a specter in the halls. The apparition is believed to be someone who died at the site during the inn's heyday.

According to manager Stella Blaise, even a newly arrived resident complains of hearing somebody walking up and down the corridor at night. Although Stella has worked at the housing complex for 14 years, she's yet to experience any paranormal despite residents complaining *all the time* of the relentless footsteps.

POTTERSVILLE

THE WELLS HOUSE

Early Warren County chronicles relate how travelers bound for Schroon Lake were met at the train station and transported by stagecoach to the Potters Hotel. Built in 1845, the North Country inn offered authentic Adirondack hospitality. Guests dined on fresh lake trout for breakfast and woodland venison for dinner.

After lunch, summer folks boarded *The Evelyn* which steamed up Schroon Lake from Pottersville stopping at other lakefront lodges.

New proprietors, John B. Wells and his wife Alida M. Bibby, changed the hotel's name to the Wells House. Fishermen and hunters sidled up to the oak bar to trade fish tales and brag about the "one that got away." Local farmers smiled knowingly over a cold beer.

In 2005 the hotel, located at 6 Olmstedville Road, underwent a major overhaul converting the hostelry's 22 rooms into 11 modern rooms and suites. When a building is revamped, the transformation can sometimes "wake-up" the dormant spirits. Ghosts, like their living counterparts, do not take kindly to unexpected changes in their environment. According to David Pitkin's account in *New York State Ghosts, Volume Two*, it was during the massive renovation that "screwy" things started to occur.

When co-owner Marian McCann went to change a burned-out light bulb she found the bulb merely unscrewed. Since she needed a ladder to reach the socket, she found the incident baffling. This anomaly continuously occurs.

Some guests hear people talking and laughing outside their rooms. Staffers say they discern music and dancing in the café. Presumably the revelry harkens back to the days when festive square dancers strutted their stuff in the space.

Apparitions are the rarest supernatural phenomenon. Most ghosts will hardly ever make themselves known unless they detect a person who is intuitive or psychically open. Children's ghosts, on the other hand, seek companionship and/or some form of parental energy. The ghost of a little girl shows up in the Wells House from time to time. The vision of her enchanting sprite delights visitors.

An oft-told legend that floats to the surface on occasion concerns a woman who was murdered in the bathtub when her husband caught her cheating on him. The tall tale only adds to the lodge's spooky allure.

(Photo courtesy The BrightSide on Raquette).

RAQUETTE LAKE

THE BRIGHTSIDE
ON RAQUETTE

Raquette Lake is located in the heart of the Adirondack Mountains. The Brightside Hotel was built on the lake's Indian Point in 1891. Frank Giotto and The Light Connection purchased the property in 2001 for their clients' use, meetings and training sessions.

Accessible only by boat the Brightside Hotel closed decades ago, but was a popular destination in the early 1900s.

Joseph O. A. Bryere migrated from Canada and in 1884, married Mary Agnes Gooley at the "Under the Hemlocks" inn located at Long Point on Raquette Lake. During the first year of their marriage they lived in a tent while constructing their lakeside hotel. Eventually they developed a complex of "Great Camp" style buildings—cabins, a boathouse and a water tower comprised a 100-acre wilderness retreat.

The Brightside boasted modern amenities, water sports, tennis courts, hiking and golf at the nearby links—visitors hailed the resort as heaven on earth.

In Joe's carpenter shop over the boathouse

he produced exceptional Adirondack-style furniture—many of these one-of-a-kind pieces are displayed at the Adirondack Museum in Blue Mountain Lake.

Their four children snowshoed across the lake to school at the J. Pierpont Morgan estate on Long Point in winter. In the spring and fall, they traveled via guide boat.

As with many old buildings, tales of ghosts always intrigue and the Brightside has come by quite a few over the years. On numerous occasions, guests insist they felt, witnessed, or simply "knew" there was *something* there.

When blue spheres of light floated about one of the bedrooms, the resident guest admitted his fright. He felt too embarrassed to leave his room, so afraid he'd show his fear. The next morning he dismissed everything that he *thought* happened until he began to view the Mohawk Valley Ghost Hunters photo file. In some of the shots, he observed the same orbs in the pictures that he perceived the night before.

A female guest insisted that as she made her bed she heard what sounded like her camera snapping photos. She kept regarding the camera, which sat on the dresser. The developed film exhibited three identical pictures of the room including the mysterious bluish orbs of light.

This unit has been dubbed the "ghost room" and is obviously the most actively paranormal location at the BrightSide. One overnight guest actually became angry when asked if he slept well the night before. He claimed the dresser drawers banged opened and closed and along with the fan that spun from extremely fast to slow, greatly irritated the guest because he thought the staff was playing a joke on him.

Another guest in the same room woke up to the sound of the fan racing. He turned his light on but all seemed well. Unable to fall back asleep, he read until growing drowsy. He eventually settled down to sleep and as soon as he put his head on the pillow he felt the pillow flatten next to his head as if someone rested *their* head on his pillow as well. He immediately leaped out of the bed.

The Brightside on Raquette's third floor is actively haunted. Alarms sound simultaneously, beds shake, windows rattle and, most startlingly, the image of a woman appears in a mirror!

Kim Teesdale's best friend and colleague experienced something so staggering that he waited one year to inform her of the encounter. Kim's friend said as he quieted down toward sleep, he sensed something in the room with him. Opening his eyes, he observed an image of an incorporeal blue dress floating in the room. He explained the dress looked like it belonged to a young girl. He put his head under the covers until morning and tried to convince himself the harrowing experience was an awful dream. Why did he wait one year to tell Kim? The incident *still* haunts him to this day so he finally felt compelled to share the eerie occurrence with her.

Another guest who stayed in the ghost room awoke to find an ephemeral woman in a white dress standing over him. He kept mum about what happened until others shared their own ghost stories from the past.

Another time, a New York investigator, who asked to stay in the scariest room, ended up on the couch downstairs. The investigator said he fled the third floor room immediately because he became overwhelmed with depression as soon as he entered the space.

Who is haunting the BrightSide on Raquette? Some say the spirit is Bryere's sister-in-law. The earliest ghost story involves she and her husband who stayed in one of the bedrooms over the kitchen in the 1970s.

Despite a blinding blizzard, the husband set out for the village over the frozen lake and never returned. His faithful wife kept vigil, gazing out the window and awaiting his return. He never did. Some feel her spirit refuses to check out. As if on cue, when someone plays the old, original Vose and Sons piano in the Great Room a female apparition appears. Psychics contend the music comforts the grieving, ghostly woman.

In 2001, during renovation, workers found a woman's coat hanging on the wall in the Great Room. The vintage coat appeared to be in pristine condition. They left the garment hanging there. A few months later, a man's coat, from the same era, mysteriously appeared on the hook next to it. No one knows where, when or how the garment got there.

Maybe it was a prank, but then again, maybe her husband, after all these years, finally came home...

To sum it up, I feel Kim Teesdale says it best: "The Brightside is intriguing, mystical and full of history and one of the most beautiful places in the Adirondacks to visit. I enjoy hearing these [ghost] stories. I enjoy the stories because I get to hear them first hand, but the best part is watching their facial expressions and eyes widen as the story is told. Sometimes, I don't hear the story right away because I think they don't really believe what happened or that it may have been a dream."

THE TAP ROOM

After a disastrous 1927 fire consumed much of the village, the present Raquette Lake Supply Company building was rebuilt on Main Street. The Tap Room is housed in the vintage structure and the popular watering hole has been "lifting spirits in Raquette Lake" for many years.

On a hot summer day there's nothing better than an ice cold beer to quench the thirst. The Tap Room offers rooms upstairs which is a good thing for those who over imbibe. There are those who "slept it off" in a room above the bar and awoke to a startling vision, although they thought it a dream. Some long term tenants *know* however that what they saw was real, yet not of this world.

Although Room 15 now functions as a storage room there was a time when it was available to rent. The strange goings on in that chamber terminated any type of lease, permanently.

On several occasions, a former Tap Room employee witnessed the apparition of a woman wearing a vintage, flowered dress. The worker resided upstairs for a time and one night her neighbor across the hall frantically beat on her door to let him in.

"There's a woman in my room and she won't leave," he gasped.

"He was scared out of his mind," she told me. "He curled up in a fetal position and rocked in my chair."

Others hear the woman's voice. A psychic discerned the ghostly woman who stays behind is waiting for someone to return—most likely her World War II soldier sweetheart.

(Photo courtesy of Cindy Higby).

WELLSCROFT LODGE

The Wellscroft Lodge was built in 1903 as a summer home for Jean and Wallis Craig Smith of Michigan. The Smiths enjoyed the home for many years until they lost their fortune in the stock market crash.

The most recent owners, Linda and Randolph Stanley, ran the 1890 Tudor Revival Mansion as a bed and breakfast inn. During their residency, the house possessed friendly spirits.

Although no radio existed on the property, guests often discerned gentle, instrumental melodies emanating from different parts of the house. Disconcerting murmurings were heard, although indistinguishable. Most mysterious is the "lady in red." She is spotted gazing out the front window or gliding down the staircase.

At the time of its construction upon Ebenezer Mountainside, the Wellscroft Lodge was one of the largest estates built in the Adirondacks. Its English Tudor style was modeled after a Scottish home the Smiths admired.

The 17,000 square foot mansion included

a community of buildings to support the family's every imaginable need. An all-important caretaker's house existed along with the power house, ice house, carriage house and stables. Gardens, a children's playhouse, golf course and even a maple syrup house buoyed up the enclave. Given the couples' iron-ore and timber industry fortune, no expense was spared.

Like so many others, the 1929 economic downturn crushed the Smith's lavish existence. Sold in 1942, various owners possessed the massive property over the next 50 years. The structure saw incarnations as a private home, a public resort and eventually sat abandoned. The sadly neglected home that once housed genial family gatherings, convivial parties and children's laughter became the victim of vandals.

The Stanleys took on the onerous task of restoring the great manse to its original splendor. During their residency as innkeepers guests often mentioned to their hosts how they enjoyed the beautiful music wafting through the structure. Visitors also often heard the noise of disembodied revelers coming in the front door along with the distinct sound of the heavy, creaking door opening and closing.

Stanley family members and workers hired to help with the restoration also experienced supernatural anomalies. One of the painters never returned to finish the job because he was so freaked out. The painter's behavior is in contrast to a caretaker's spirit who stays behind long after the completion of his earthly tasks. His ghost is spotted outside traipsing between the fire house and the power house. He is recognized by his unusual wide-brimmed hat.

Another spirit sighted is a former servant who stands with his arms crossed at the entrance to the third floor servants' quarters.

*This photo captured light orbs where one person claimed to see a spirit.
(Photo courtesy of Brian Dominic).*

Without doubt the Lady in Red is the star
of this haunted house. Her ghost glides down
the grand staircase and passersby observe
her eerie presence peering out a second

floor window of the "green room" as well. Her appearance identifies her as a turn-of-the century Victorian woman. Mrs. Stanley actually noticed physical impressions on the window seat cushions, allegedly left by the lady of the house.

When Mrs. Stanley contacted a psychic, the medium immediately discerned a woman in a red dress sitting by the window watching and waiting for someone. In the 1960s, a previous owner also observed her floating down the staircase!

The well-crafted Wellscroft Lodge offers breathtaking views, incomparable serenity and remarkable presences from the past.

WILTON

ULYSSES S. GRANT COTTAGE

Duncan McGregor purchased Palmertown Mountain from New York State in a tax sale in 1872. He built a small resort and restaurant for summer visitors on the peak he renamed Mount McGregor.

Ten years later, Joseph Drexel, a wealthy Philadelphia financier, bought the property. Drexel razed the small hotel and opened a more sumptuous resort, the Hotel Balmoral. He financed a 10.5-mile narrow-gauge railroad from Saratoga Springs to the top of the mountain. The railroad brought men and supplies up the slope to build the grand hotel and in succeeding summers delivered workers and guests.

Fire destroyed the fashionable resort in 1897 and was never rebuilt. The area's popularity faded and the railroad crumbled.

Metropolitan Life Insurance opened the "sanitarium on the mountain" in 1913 for its employees. The company constructed a tuberculosis center consisting of about 30 buildings and established farms at the foot of the mountain to sustain the complex. This sanitarium, fully staffed by doctors and nurses worked to restore the health of all the company's employees.

In 1945, Governor Dewey purchased the site as a rest camp for World War II veterans until the 1950s when the complex served as an annex to the Rome State School, eventually renamed the Wilton Developmental Center. The Adirondack-style "Grant Cottage" sits yards from Mount McGregor's summit. The rocking chairs on the porch help the cottage look much as it did when Ulysses S. Grant resided there.

In 1885, President Grant was given a terminal diagnosis and struggled to finish his memoirs. Drexel offered the president use of his personal cottage and some rooms in the hotel. The Grant entourage, including family members, servants and physicians arrived on June 16th. On July 23rd, four days after Grant completed his manuscript he passed away and was waked in the parlor.

In 1900, Governor Theodore Roosevelt declared the cottage a New York State Historic Site.

Today, the Friends of the Ulysses S. Grant Cottage operate the museum. The cottage remains the same as during Grant's stay. Visitors view the original furnishings and the president's personal items, including the bed where he died. Even (dried) floral arrangements remain from Grant's funeral.

Although President Grant died in the dwelling he is not the one haunting the premises. It's a female apparition who is sometimes spotted inside or out on the grounds. Her specter is presumed to be a former caretaker, still deeply devoted to tending the historic home. Corrections Officer Scott M. Mitchell, who works at the Mount McGregor Correctional Facility, observed a male phantom walking around the building. He felt this spirit looked after the site as well.

MOUNT MCGREGOR
CORRECTIONAL FACILITY

Since the mid-1970s, the property surrounding the Ulysses S. Grant Cottage serves as the Mount McGregor Correctional Facility, a minimum-medium security men's prison. The mountaintop itself is now a wire-enclosed playing field.

The correctional facility is plagued by visions of many spirits, though the most noted is a small girl with curly blonde hair. She appears to be between six and eight years of age and she is spotted peering out of the prison windows or standing in a high-security area.

Scott Mitchell claims to play hide 'n seek with the youngster who always wears the same pleated, pinafore dress. Attuned to the spiritual side of life, his Native American traditions enable him to perceive things invisible to others.

A chilling paranormal event occurred in Building #10 one blistering July day. Mitchell said the second floor felt so cold it was as if the air conditioner blew full blast *except* there is no A/C in the building! As a fellow female officer secured the door, the glass window exploded. The entity who "punched" the thick glass left a hole that looked like a fist went through it. "He's *mean*," Mitchell emphasized. The notorious presence is commonly known and co-workers nervously joke about it. Could this unseen entity be a former inmate or an old veteran, perhaps traumatized by war?

Mitchell also mentioned several co-workers on their way to work observed an ephemeral woman in white walking along the road at the base of the mountain. Possibly another revenant of the carefree days at Mount McGregor.

Acknowledgments

Only one name appears on the cover but it "took a village" to write this third volume of Adirondack ghost stories. Every person I spoke with was pleasantly forthcoming and generous with their time, information and, in some cases, photos. I'd like to recognize all who assisted me:

Joanne Baldwin, Deer's Head Inn; Loretta Bates, Washington County Deputy Historian; Stella Blaise, Lee House Apartments; Barbara Brassard, Ticonderoga Chamber of Commerce; Cliff and Jean Bruce, The Village Booksmith; Cano Davy and Marcus Zwierecki, New York State Paranormal Research; Brian Dominic, Century 21 Foote-Ryan Real Estate; James Dunning; Jim Emerson, D.V.M.; Marie Gandron, Hudson Falls Library; Margaret Gibbs, Adirondack History Center Museum; Joyce Haag, Town of Webb Historical Association; Cathy Higby; Rebecca Humrich, Sheridan Books; Joan Hunsdon, Crown Point

Historian; Hannelore Kissam, Crary Foundation; Tony Leiker, Albedor Great Camp; Peg Masters; R. Paul McCarty, Fort Edward Historian; Scott M. Mitchell, a.k.a. "Two Blankets;" Bob Muller, Glenmore Bar & Grill; Greg Pakarklis; Rosemary Remington, Stoneleigh Bed & Breakfast; Linda Roy, John Brown Farm; Thomas Scozzafava, Moriah Town Supervisor; Kim Teesdale, Fiber Instrument Sales and Frank Giotto, The Light Company and BrightSide on Raquette; Deb Tremper, Six Penny Graphics; Dayna Winters, ISIS Paranormal Investigations; and Mike Yost, Sheridan Books.

A special acknowledgment to my friends… Mary and George Baer for welcoming me for over 25 years. Thank you too, Mary, for navigating mountain roads in pursuit of photos. To Rick Baer and Robyn Brown for your company and contribution, Susan and Cornelius Burke for delightful dining experiences, Pamela and Danny Garber for your artistic input and my sounding board Maryann "Mare" Way for fine-tuning the manuscript.

Sincere thanks to you all!

Bibliography

Allen, Martha. "Is Keene Valley Haunted?" *Lake Placid News*; June 6, 2008.

Clarke, Martha. *General Grant on Mount McGregor*. Transcribed handwritten document by the wife of the first caretaker of the Grant Cottage. Undated.

Cobb, Stephen. "Believe it or Not, The Ghosts of Paul Smith's College." *The Sequel*; Fall 2004.

Conrad, Jennifer. "20 Haunted Hotels." *Woman's Day*; July 2008.

De la Rocha, Kelly. "Olde Knox Mansion in Johnstown reputed to be home to ghosts." *The Daily Gazette*; October 26, 2008.

Delarue, John. "The Adirondack's Oldest Inn." www.4peaks.com

"Ghost Story Runs Wild at Dannemora." *Chateaugay Record*; March 18, 1931.

"Grace Brown's Ghost Seen." *The Plattsburgh Sentinel*; July 16, 1909.

Gruse, Doug. "Group tracks ghosts of librarians past." *Post Star*; April 17, 2009.

Hogan, R. Craig, Ph.D. *Your Eternal Self*. Greater Reality Publications; 2008.

"Home News." *Chateaugay Journal*; October 8, 1897.

"Home News." *Chateaugay Journal*; October 14, 1897.

Lipson, Eden Ross. "Day Trip; A General's Final Retreat." *The New York Times*; July 30, 2004.

Macken, Lynda Lee. *Adirondack Ghosts*. Black Cat Press; 2000.

_____. *Adirondack Ghosts II.* Black Cat Press; 2004.

"Malone's Mystery." *Chateaugay Journal;* October 18, 1897.

Manchester, Lee. "The Resurrection of Wellscroft." *Adirondack Life;* September/October 2002.

_____. "Iron Center Museum tells story of Moriah mills & mines." *Lake Placid News;* October 24, 2003.

_____. "A tour of three historic Adirondack inns, rescued from oblivion." *Lake Placid News;* April 7, 2006.

McKinstry, Lohr. "Adirondack Haunts." *Press Republican;* October 27, 2007.

_____. "Supernatural Shorts." *Press Republican;* October 27, 2007.

McLaughlin, Bill. "Park Street Beat, About Tupper Lake." *Adirondack Daily Enterprise;* February 4, 1954.

Pitkin, David J. *New York State Ghosts, Volume 1.* Aurora Publications; 2006.

_____. *New York State Ghosts, Volume Two.* Aurora Publications; 2008.

"Placid Reflections—Spooky Happenings in Upper Jay!" *Placid Thoughts,* Issue #003, October 7, 2007; www.lake-placid-area-guide.com.

Revai, Cheri. *More Haunted Northern New York.* North Country Books; 2003.

_____. *The Big Book of New York Ghost Stories.* Stackpole Books; 2009.

Rico, Antonieta. "Northern New York offers haunts for ghost seekers." *The Mountaineer Online;* October 28, 2004.

Subar, Zach. "Knox Mansion ready for Halloween." *The Leader-Herald;* October 31, 2009.

Untitled. *Franklin Gazette;* October 5, 1897.

Williams, Donald R. *Along the Adirondack Trail.* Arcadia Publishing; 2004.

Web Resources

Adirondack Architectural Heritage: www.aarch.org

Albedor: www.albedor.com

The BrightSide on Raquette: www.brightsideonraquette.com

Covewood Lodge: www.covewoodlodge.com

Essex County Historical Society/Adirondack History Center Museum: www.adkhistorycenter.org

Glenmore Bar & Grill: www.glenmorebarandgrill.com

Hudson Falls Free Library: www.hudsonfalls.sals.edu

ISIS Paranormal Investigations: www.isisinvestigations.com

John Brown Farm State Historic Site: www.nysparks.state.ny.us/historic-sites

Paul Smith's College: www.paulsmiths.edu

Penfield Foundation in Ironville, NY: www.penfieldmuseum.org

Saratoga County Archival Record Index: www. saratoga.5points.net

The Shadowlands: www.theshadowlands.net

Spectral Review: www.spectralreview.com

Stoneleigh Bed and Breakfast: www.stoneleighbedandbreakfast.com

Town of Webb Historical Association: www.webbhistory.org

Ulysses S. Grant Cottage: www.grantcottage.org

The Wells House: www.wellshouse.com

Wikipedia: www.wikipedia.com

Also by Lynda Lee Macken

Adirondack Ghosts

Adirondack Ghosts II

Empire Ghosts

Ghostly Gotham

Ghosts of Central New York

Ghosts of the Garden State

Ghosts of the Garden State II

Ghosts of the Garden State III

Haunted Baltimore

Haunted Cape May

Haunted History of Staten Island

Haunted Houses
of the Hudson Valley

Also by Lynda Lee Macken

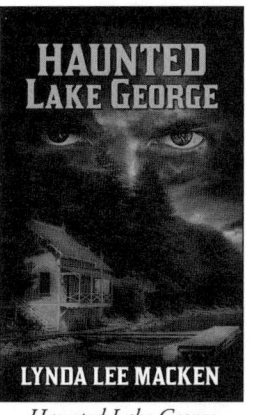
Haunted Lake George

Haunted Long Island

Haunted Long Island II

Haunted New Hope

Haunted Salem & Beyond

Array of Hope